Psychology *in*

Downton Abbey

Season 1

Psychology in

Downton Abbey

Season 1

Copyright © 2013 by Louella Chapman

Table of Contents

Acknowledgements

"We stand on the shoulders of giants" – Isaac Newton

My giants :

My dear friend Joan Engelhaupt who spent countless hours - beyond the call of duty - reading and critiquing my draft and enabling me to move from draft to next-version-draft

My dear colleague Ann Palik who made sure my psychological references made psychological sense

My husband, my Downton Abbey couch-potato buddy. He also lent his time, critiquing my book and supporting my dream of writing this book throughout.

My son, who inspires me to be better

Thank you for your sturdy shoulders!

Introduction

My husband and I didn't start watching Downton Abbey until the beginning of Season 2 and after a couple of episodes, I was hooked! It always helps to have attractive actors and actresses play the main characters like Dan Stevens as Matthew Crawley and Michelle Dockery as Lady Mary. They make us want to keep looking at them and therefore we are captivated. Add to that the romantic uber-feminine fashion with laces, jeweled-gowns, and satin gloves; plus the grandeur of the home, its furnishings and the estate elicit nostalgia. But for a "student" of psychology like me, it was the exquisite dialogue, the characterizations that were consistent and made sense psychologically, that grabbed me immediately. And even though this show is primarily character-driven, the plot and sub-plots also hold together very well. My hats are off to Julian Fellowes, creator of Downton Abbey for his genius as a writer. The dribbling of the characters' back stories neatly tie up loose ends too.

The show and Season One opens with the catastrophic sinking of the supposedly-unsinkable mighty Titanic in 1912, and the death of an important passenger to the Crawleys, set the wheels in motion of this first season.

Although this is a period drama, set in the early 20th century, most of the themes and issues that are portrayed are still relevant today. There are still hierarchies in societies, sex is still controversial, siblings still vie for attention, and loves and lovers of all shapes and forms still abound. I grew up in modern times, but in a traditional society. Although I have a brother, I have four sisters and the dynamics in this all-girl family struck a familiar chord in me. Most of all, Lady Mary, being the oldest, and her felt obligation to take care of her family tugged my heart as my oldest sister had a similar felt role in her life. I dedicate this book to my Ate.

I will discuss several psychological phenomena I have observed in Downton Abbey, Season 1. You'll get a smorgasbord of my interpretations of the drives, motivations and behaviors of the different personalities involved as well as the forces from the environment that play into their lives. I hope you get to enjoy the show more after reading my book.

Attachment

The psychiatrist John Bowlby theorized that the emotional bonds (also known as attachments) that we have with our significant others in early childhood (and I will stretch this to significant things, objects or places later) affect the quality of our relationships and lives in general. Caregivers who are attentive and responsive help build a sense of security in children, enabling them to have an internal safe haven or secure base. They feel that the world is a safe place. On the other hand, an unpredictable or undependable caregiver creates anxiety in children and they learn not to trust the world.

Bowlby, born 1907, was English. He was a sensitive boy who, at age four, lost the nanny who had practically raised him. Typical of mothers of the nobility during that time, his own mother spent only about an hour a day with him. He was also sent to a boarding school at the tender age of seven and he later confessed that he suffered from all that separation. Although this was not unusual for the upper class British during that era, these experiences of loss and separation fueled his theories about human attachments and how they influence personality.

The Earl of Grantham, Robert Crawley, is not a particularly warm person. We see that in his relationship with his mother, Dowager Countess of Grantham, Violet Crawley, there is actually a great deal of tension between them as he seems annoyed by her quite a bit (Later on we would realize that, like John Bowlby above, Robert's mother also just spent about an hour a day with him while he was a child and a nanny took care of him for the rest of the time (Perhaps he was also sent to a boarding school eventually!). In fact, it seems as if Robert is more emotionally attached to Downton Abbey, the estate, than to his own mother as he speaks tenderly about his home and how it has affected him. He admits to his mother that Downton's nurturing of him, and this nurture of the estate, is "like having a third parent and a fourth child". No wonder it seems his whole energy is devoted to saving this estate, which he clearly loves; sometimes it seems even more so than his own children. Lady Mary once complained to him that "it seems like you are the only one who is not fighting for me," as it relates to Robert's reluctance to fight the entail. (This means that the fortune that Cora, Mary's mother, brought into the marriage is tied into the estate and that the heir of Downton will inherit that too.)

Lady Mary actually has a special relationship with the butler, Mr. Carson. Carson took care of Mary when she was little and loves her as if she were his own child. "We're all behind you Lady Mary," Carson says as he tries to soothe Lady Mary when he sensed that she was in the dumps. That sums up how Carson treats her – He's got her back! So many times, we see Lady Mary opening up to Carson when she is emotionally distressed instead of to her own parents. She knows that Carson can give her the comfort and soothing that her parents are not capable of doing. Mary feels safe with Carson. A few times we've seen Lady Mary crying on Carson's shoulders. With Carson's arms around her, his face is mirroring the pain she is feeling. Mirroring here means reflecting Lady Mary's feelings back to her or empathizing with her. When we empathize with another (suffering) person, we somehow help alleviate his or her suffering as the person feels less burdened having shared with someone.

Cora Levinson Crawley, Countess of Grantham and wife of Robert, is American and a little more expressive than the Crawleys. She is the mother of their three daughters: Lady Mary, Lady Edith and Lady Sybil. Yet she also does not seem to have a strong emotional attachment, nor is she tuned in to any of her daughters. This may be explained by her own strained relationship with her own mother. You see, her mother, like a lot of *nouveau riche* American families at that time, wanted their children to marry into the British nobility. Cora was only twenty when she married Robert (who was then eighteen), and their marriage was something akin to an arranged marriage. She was young and must have felt forced into a life and family in a foreign country that may have been hard to adapt and assimilate to. In the same way that Cora's mother did not tune in to her, she also has a lot to learn as far as getting to know her three children, all very different from each other. For example, she did not realize that it was actually Lady Edith who was in love with Patrick Crawley, their second cousin who died when the Titanic sank, and not Lady Mary, who was engaged to him.

We also see Cora eats her breakfast in bed. The first waking hours of a child are so important to the bonding experience at a young age as the "separation" during the night can be terrifying to small children. However, Cora submitted to this tradition of the English culture, not knowing any other way to be – a young mother on her own in a foreign land. I will speculate that this affected the quality of the children's bond with her.

Arranged Marriages

Cora and Robert's marriage was sort of like an arranged marriage – an arrangement that's good for their families-of-origin, an invisible contract between them to suit their needs. It fulfills Cora's family's need to be part of the British nobility and Robert's family's need to save Downton Abbey from financial ruin. Nevertheless, after a year, Robert claims to have fallen in love with Cora. So the arranged marriage blossomed into romantic love.

At this point in the story, Robert's history is becoming Lady Mary's story. Once again, Downton Abbey needs to be rescued. But because Cora and Robert did not produce an heir (they had no son), none of their daughters could inherit Downton Abbey by English law. Worse than that, the money that Cora brought into the marriage cannot be separated from the entail as Robert's father set it up that way, as he assumed that Cora and Robert were going to have a son. As a result, the Crawley daughters are doomed to be penniless.

Mary, being the oldest and the prettiest, has the burden to save and keep Downton Abbey for her family by marrying the heir (distant cousins Patrick - until the Titanic sank - and Matthew) or marrying a rich noble Englishman – another arrangement. Cora, the mother, having been in the same predicament in the past as far as saving Downton Abbey, takes an important role in matchmaking for Lady Mary. She took special interest in Evelyn Napier and later encouraged Mary and Matthew to wed. (Parents' antennas become sharp when they have marriageable daughters - and sons to a lesser extent. They are anxious that their children will not make a wise choice, and they try to steer them towards what they think is the right direction.) Although arranged or pseudo-arranged marriages were not far from the norm during those times, there must be some foreboding felt by Lady Mary whenever she is being set up with an unlikely beau. To not be able to control who you will spend the rest of your life with – Wow! - must create a panic in others.

Research these days by the way shows that arranged marriages last longer than romantic or "love" marriages. If the only criteria to determine success in marriages is staying together or not separating, then arranged marriages seem to have a higher success rate. If you think about it, in arranged or "forced" marriages, it is also implied that you are forced to make it work, you have no choice. So you work harder to achieve that working relationship. Whereas in love marriages, it's your choice to marry whomever and perhaps psychically, you also think it's your choice to stay or not. The expectations are lower.

Heirs

"Downton Abbey," being the title of this show, is apt, as it seems like the why and wherefore of most of the characters is to keep Downton Abbey, the estate, at all costs (This reminds me of "Gone with the Wind" and Scarlett O' Hara's devotion to their estate, "Tara").

At that time, one of the most important achievements of a couple from the nobility was to produce a son, an heir. Why this is an "achievement" is so that the bloodline of succession continues, and property stays within their circle (a survival necessity), add to that carrying their last name into perpetuity. So imagine the dilemma (and disappointment) that Robert and Cora – and of course Violet – had that they only have daughters. Cora was forced to sign an entail by her father-in-law to ensure that Downton Abbey and her dowry would be handed down to their progeny. This is because her father-in-law assumed that they would have a son.

Until Cora was close to menopausal age, not having a son was probably not a matter of concern. But as she got closer to that stage, the anxiety kicked in and finding an heir became so paramount. There were a few potential fiance candidates, until third cousin, Matthew Crawley came into the scene. He slowly became a favorite of Robert. Sometime during his training period (regarding the business of the estate) with Robert, Robert started enjoying him like his own son. Robert also started respecting Matthew's integrity. Robert must have felt like he finally had the son he'd always wanted! Mary believes he has always wished for a son, which is not far-fetched. She gets jealous over Robert's close relationship with Matthew later.

Close to the end of Season 1, Cora becomes pregnant and hopes that she will deliver a natural heir were rekindled. This would later play a minor role in Mary's hesitancy to accept Matthew's marriage proposal. And so it was interesting to see the depth of Robert's grief due to Cora's miscarriage after Dr. Clarkson confirmed that Cora was expecting a boy!

Intrusive In-laws

Violet Crawley, mother of Robert, is intrusive and takes on the task of saving Downton as her own personal goal, even if it means quarrelling with other stakeholders such as Cora every now and then. Cora and Robert have a "knowing look" whenever Violet is announced to be visiting. Losing Downton would mean losing the only thing – a place – that gives Violet her life's meaning and where she gets to exercise power. This power is very important to her, as feeling and looking powerful allows her to hide her insecurity. (More on this later)

Violet also doesn't seem to have scruples. That is one more manifestation of how she exercises her power. She consulted Matthew (behind Robert's back) about Matthew's OWN potential inheritance and how he could perhaps see if it could be broken. Granted that she had good intentions (that is to see if something else can be done so as not to leave the girls destitute), this should really be an issue between the generations below her.

One time, when Cora was scolded by Robert in Violet's presence, Cora was irked: "Of course, it gave your mother her best evening since Christmas", meaning that Violet felt victorious over Cora. But Cora is tolerating and even enabling Violet's intrusion into their lives. She often tells her the minutiae of Mary's prospects and activities. She gives Violet the impression that Violet's opinions are valued. Cora could just inform Violet every now and then as a matter-of-fact.

Violet was not the only intrusive in-law. Her husband, Cora's father-in-law forced Cora to sign the entail soon after or before her marriage to Robert. Cora resents them for this. The truth is, Violet was not in favor of Robert marrying Cora but Violet was rebuffed by Violet's own husband. Now Cora has the makings of an intrusive in-law as well with the way she is so involved in Mary's suitors. It's interesting however, that she does not seem as concerned with her other daughters' lives. We will learn later that it's because of a scandal that involves Lady Mary and her felt need to cover that up.

Here's another example of a good-intentioned but bordered on the intrusive intervention: When Cora was pregnant towards the end of Season 1, Lady Rosamund, sister of Robert and aunt to Cora's daughters, suggested to Lady Mary to postpone accepting Matthew's marriage proposal until they find out if Cora would be delivering an heir. Lady Rosamund planted a doubt in Lady Mary's mind that Lady Mary may become bored being married to a mere solicitor, if Matthew does not become heir of Downton Abbey.

Intrusive in-laws are more common in collectivist societies where individuals who marry still have a hard time transferring their loyalty to their new spouses and their divided loyalty seems "for sale". But intrusive in-laws also happen if the in-laws have a hard time separating from their children even after their marriages. Or perhaps they don't have separate lives with their own interests. Or that their own marriages are out of kilter, and so they continue to use their (married) children as buffers between them and their spouses.

Individuation

There is a stage of development we call individuation. That is when an individual tries to become his or her own person and remove the tether between him or herself and his or her parents. This usually starts sometime in adolescence and actually continues on throughout life. I'm not sure that anyone really achieves 100% or total individuation as the stakes are usually too high to do that - especially in cultures where group loyalty is a virtue. A "reference point" from birth, parents – to some extent - retains that role in their children's lives.

Are mothers really more conflicted than fathers in letting go of their children – as they individuate and live their own lives? For mothers, children at one time were literally "the same" as them in flesh for nine months. And for several years, children were completely dependent on their parents or caregivers. So parents' brains have been programmed for 365 days a year, for about 18 years that their children are incapable of living their lives without their doting presence. As children become more independent, the dependency factor lowers and most parents start to relax. But then adolescence and its accompanying budding sexuality emerge and the fear factor kicks in again. Especially for daughters as after all, it is girls who get pregnant. "No one's sensible at her age. Nor should they be. That's our job"- Robert comments regarding Mary's choice for a mate. Although not related to this issue, Robert at one time also commented "... But we must have a care for feminine sensibilities. They are finer and more fragile than our own." Robert does not trust that Mary is capable of making sensible choices, even though Mary was twenty-four. He himself, at an even younger age of eighteen, was forced to marry Cora, age twenty then. During the first year of Robert and Cora's marriage, he must have been miserable as he was not in love with Cora. That first-year experience must be indelible in his mind, and he is afraid to have Mary experience the same vicissitude.

Robert Crawley also struggles with launching his children. He also does not know his children very well. He considers himself the head of the household and the authority. But times are changing for women, and he does not realize that his daughter Sybil has become very political, thanks to the influence of their chauffeur, Tom Branson. They are also living in an era of dramatic political storms especially feminism and the Irish Republican movement. So when Sybil attended a political meeting without his knowledge (and got hurt in the process), Robert indignantly said: "Which is why I am astonished you should not feel it necessary to ask my permission to attend." He does not like Sybil challenging his authority.

He feels threatened by that. As we see here, Sybil is a product of her time. Feminism lubricated the way to individuation for women.

Cora, on the other hand, says, "You build up your dreams for your children. And then... fate just smashes them to pieces"- after Mary's scandal involving Kemal Pamuk (More on this later). Cora is disappointed that Mary is trying to live her own life, not Cora's ideal life for Mary. Some say that once a mother, you wear your heart on your sleeve forever. Cora is worried that Mary will suffer endlessly as a result of the indiscretion that happened. And for a mother, this thought is unbearable. So she participates very actively in trying to steer Mary's life from that point, hoping to subvert fate, forgetting that it really is only Mary in the end who will live her own life.

William, the footman, was an only child, as all of his siblings died in infancy. He wanted to be a groom as he loved horses but his mother had different plans for him. She wanted him to be a footman as this is a stepping stone towards becoming a butler. William decides to please his mother rather than to pursue his own dream. She is proud of him for getting the job at Downton Abbey. William is very close to his mother and was homesick initially. "If you're feeling homesick, there's no shame in it. It means you come from a happy home. "There's plenty of people here who'd envy that," said Mrs. Hughes to William. With William giving up his dream of becoming a groom and instead taking on the footman-to-butler route to please his mother, we can see that individuation was not something his mother valued. William may have expressed something to his mother about his preferred occupation but was perhaps shut down by her. Mother loomed large over his life. William was torn. I am guessing that his mother believed that taking the footman-to-butler route was a more stable endeavor as it implies more job security. So it's her fear (and love) for William's future that was a driving factor, without consideration for what William really wanted. And we all know the power of our parents' approval or disapproval. But William is only 23 and it's possible that future life experiences will spur him to detour from his mother's chosen path.

Matthew, on the other hand, is his own person. He says, "I'm not a puppet. I must take charge of my own life." His mother, who was a nurse and the social worker-type must have the mind of a psychologist and raised Matthew to be an independent person. She must have had enough self-esteem to have allowed Matthew to separate from her and individuate, and she not be threatened by that. In fact, Matthew is so self-reliant that he resented being tended to by

Molesley, the valet assigned to him by the Granthams. (This is also due to Matthew's resistance to the trappings of being part of the elite).

It is harder for families who struggled or are struggling financially to let their children individuate. They need their children to help them survive. If they leave their families, even if only psychologically, unconsciously the family is afraid that that will lead to physical separation which is tantamount to economic separation as well. (Except of course for emigrants who send remittances home and who emigrated specifically to support their families.)

Birth Order

Because Mary is the oldest and the most beautiful in an all-girl family, she is used to getting a lot of attention. Somebody used to getting a lot of attention can become arrogant and snobbish as if the world owed them something, and it is hard for them to share the limelight. Lady Mary has some semblance of these qualities.

Also being the oldest, Lady Mary has the default role of being the third parent in terms of keeping the family and its possessions intact for the family. In this case, Lady Mary feels the burden of keeping Downton Abbey for them – for Violet, her parents, her sisters, herself and all those who have and will have a slice of the Robert-Cora DNA. Mary knows this responsibility and she resents it but feels powerless to run away from her role. Her life is not hers completely. She plays the game nevertheless and hopes that there will be a payoff someday.

Like a typical middle child, Lady Edith is not a leader. Although birth order dynamics certainly play a major role in her personality development, I also believe that because of the fact that her older sister Mary, deemed by most as the most beautiful among the three (aside from the fact that she is the oldest) and therefore the most marketable, played a role in Edith's self definition.

But for now, let's speculate how being the middle child affected her personality: She is the forgotten one. She is always walking in the shadow of Lady Mary. Her love objects are almost all throwaways of Mary, including Patrick, Sir Anthony Strallan and Matthew. She considers herself "unlucky" compared to Lady Mary. As a result of the attention that's being bestowed disproportionately on Lady Mary, she has grown to resent her, and when an opportunity came, she aimed to destroy her. She was fueled by jealous rage and intense rivalry.

Edith was also not supportive of Sybil's rebellion. Perhaps that's her way of desperately getting their parents' approval. She wants them to know that she is better than Sybil in their eyes as she will not rebel against them. She is oblivious to the women's rights movement. All she wants for herself is what Mary has.

Sybil is the third and youngest daughter of the Granthams and she is 18 years old at the beginning of Season 1. She is not as beautiful as her oldest sister Mary but she is passionate, and considered better-looking than Lady Edith. Being from the younger generation (even if only a few years), she was maturing and forming her beliefs when the women's movement was at the cusp of birthing in

England. Being the youngest, her parents have relaxed on her, and she does not have the burden that Lady Mary has to save their estate. She had more freedom to pursue other things that'll give meaning to her life. She is ambitious and sharp and she is determined to carve her own path.

Sibling Rivalry

There is intense rivalry between Mary and Edith, the type that makes them want to destroy each other. Like how Cain felt about Abel (Remember Cain ended up murdering Abel because Abel's offering was preferred by God over Cain's. This was tantamount to a rejection for Cain, which resulted in a narcissistic injury). Edith and Mary have "murderous" anger towards each other. Edith exposed Mary's involvement in Pamuk's death to the public. Mary, on the other hand, tricked Sir Anthony into thinking that another man would be proposing to Lady Edith in the last episode, implying to Sir Anthony that Edith was deceitful in her relationship with him. They are mean to each other.

When Mary confronted Edith about exposing Mary's secret, Edith said that the Turkish embassy had the right to know that their countryman died "in the arms of a slut". Labeling her sister a slut demonstrates how she wants to destroy Mary's reputation, almost as intense as Cain's anger towards Abel.

Edith is always eclipsed by Lady Mary. Mary is the prettier one – and therefore more marketable - and their parents are both so focused on Mary getting married, that Edith is almost invisible to them. In fact, in one of the scenes between Robert and Cora, Robert commented, "Poor old Edith; we never seem to talk about her." Lady Grantham replies: "I'm afraid Edith will be the one to care for us in our old age." So this attitude of her parents is sensed by Edith somehow, and she is desperately trying to fight for relevance in her family. Most parents don't realize how hurtful it is for a child to not be the preferred one.

Later on, after Lady Sybil's first Season in London,

Cora says to Sybil: "You were a great success in London, darling. Well done."

Edith: "You never say that to me."

Cora: "Don't I dear? You were very helpful. Thank you." (Damning with faint praise)

Compared to Lady Sybil, she is again dull while Lady Sybil is passionate.

It is understandable that Edith will be frustrated and angry that the men she's interested in (and trying to win over) are interested in her sister Mary or distracted/preoccupied by someone else while in her presence. This was how she felt when she and Matthew were visiting churches. She was almost begging for attention or for Matthew to notice her.

One of the most interesting scenes was when Edith was pleased as punch when chosen by Sir Anthony Strallan to be his date to a concert instead of Mary, in the presence of others - and especially Mary. Finally, there is someone choosing and preferring Lady Edith.

Sibling rivalry is real and powerful. If parents don't intervene, siblings will carry this into their adulthood. To intervene means to reassure each one that there's enough love and attention for all siblings. Lip service is not enough. Parents actually have to behave like they really love their children equally. Parents need to stop fights and guide them as to what is appropriate and loving behavior. Usually parents err on the side of ignoring their children's "petty" fights. Simply admonishing them and screaming, "Stop fighting!" may not do the trick. In fact, some children may feel unseen, dismissed and misunderstood by that.

Rebel (Personality type)

"Whether politically inclined like Martin Luther King, Jr., Betty Friedan, or Lech Walensa, or an artistic innovator such as Van Gogh, Joyce, or Coltrane, the Rebel is a key component of all human growth and development. The Rebel in a support group can be a powerful aid in helping the group break out of old tribal patterns. It can also help you see past tired preconceptions in your field of professional or creative endeavor. The Rebel can also lead you to reject spiritual systems that do not serve your inner need for direct union with the Divine and to seek out more appropriate paths." – Caroline Myss

Lady Sybil is this archetypal rebel and free spirit.

She is also a risk-taker. "Later you can tell them whatever you wish, but first get the job" was her advice to Gwen, and we see that she is willing to embellish the truth to achieve a goal. She is zealous and adventurous. She attended the counting of the votes for women's suffrage and insisted on staying even after Branson dissuaded her. She ended up getting hurt and put Branson's job at stake. But consistent with her determined nature, she fought for Branson to stay and threatened her own father that she would leave if Branson were fired. Her family thought she had "wild ideas" when she was just progressive. She is willing to try new things like fashion. She shocked her family when she wore harem pants.

Lady Sybil is the mover and shaker in this family. With Tom as influence, she challenges her father's authority and is real with her sisters. Although her mother is stunned initially (and of course was concerned about Lady Sybil's safety) by her moves, Cora eventually supports her (It is easier for her as she is American-bred). Robert and Violet are usually the ones opposed (at least initially) to Sybil's actions. But like Cora, Robert slowly accepts the inevitable because after all, Sybil is family. And that's usually how seemingly untraditional and unusual lifestyles (think about the gays) are eventually accepted – when it becomes personal, meaning a family member who is loved is from that group. Republican Senator Rob Portman now supports gay marriage after his own son came out of the closet and revealed he was gay. Love trumps political belief, eh?

Rebel meets political activist. Lady Sybil was intrigued by Branson's spontaneity and that was one of the ingredients in their chemistry of attraction. Tom Branson is politically-engaged and aware of the turmoil going on between Ireland and England at that time. He is not a Nelson Mandela-type freedom fighter but a feisty activist. He says, "I am a socialist, not a revolutionary." He came to Yorkshire for employment at Downton Abbey but his heart still belongs to Ireland.

On the other side of the spectrum, Carson the butler is a monarchist, loyal to and proud of the English monarchy.

One pushes forward and the other pulls back and in the end, it's usually a moderate position that wins. No wonder change takes place very slowly.

Feminism and Oppression

Had it not been for Tom Branson's entry into Downton Abbey and into Lady Sybil's life, perhaps she would not have been politicized? We don't know. She says: "I think it's terrific when people make their own lives, especially women". She had the fervor for the women's rights movement and it encompassed all women, not just her. That's why she was so involved in helping Gwen land a job as a secretary even though it meant losing a servant from their own household. She went out of her way to support Gwen's ambition by encouraging her when she was losing hope, helping with the actual job search and getting her an interview. She even took her to the interview, with her horse and buggy into town, lent her a suit, and wrote her a letter of recommendation. And lest we forget how she and Gwen dragged the horse and buggy to a blacksmith after it broke down.

Lady Sybil was also an introspective woman and questioned the differences between men and women. She protested about having to wear corsets while men didn't have to. She is excited about the changes that are happening. She said to Gwen at another time: "Things are changing for women. Not just the vote but our lives. We're going to have real lives." And to Mary, "He's not going to marry you for your looks," implying that she does not want a man to marry her for her looks – or her money.

Lady Sybil's cheer leader, Tom Branson, is a sensitive and passionate man as well. He must have felt oppressed and desperately powerless to change his life's social position. But he is smart, and his intellect will be his ticket to a better life. He is the questioning type, insightful and wants to make things right for everyone. Needless to say, social justice is important to him.

He supports Lady Sybil's passion for women's rights as he knows that oppression is the same any way one looks at it. It does not matter who's on top and who's below. It is "the same as the gap between the aristocracy and the poor." He is trying to reconcile the unfairness of having been born poor – which of course is no fault of his own – and not having the resources to move upwards. He sees the upper echelons continue to amass wealth and stave off the progress of the poor.

Another character for the same cause is petite, soft-spoken, vulnerable, and with determined-looking eyes, Rose Leslie is perfectly cast as Gwen Dawson.

She is the housemaid who fancies becoming a secretary, and secretly bought a typewriter and took a correspondence course. Her secret was exposed by (Of course!) O'Brien, and Gwen was mocked by the other servants. But like Lady Sybil, Gwen was also lucky that she was young when the women's rights movement was burgeoning. There are some cataclysmic events in history that turn stones up for us. The feminist movement was one of them and both men and women alike would be transformed by it.

I do think Lady Mary is a closet feminist herself. She supports Lady Sybil's rebellion and says Lady Sybil "might save her." Lady Mary must be thinking that if Lady Sybil can break free from the role tradition and culture has assigned to Lady Sybil, then perhaps that will apply to her too. Lady Sybil, the youngest, may pave the way for Lady Mary, the oldest, this time. Although Mary does not feel the freedom that Sybil has, of not feeling obligated to perform the role of Downton Abbey's savior, Mary says to her mother Cora "I don't believe a woman can be forced to give away all her money to a distant cousin of her husband's. Not in the 20th century. It's too ludicrous for words" referring to how Matthew may inherit her father's estate.

Virgin Mary

Lady Mary was seduced by Kemal Pamuk. Although Kemal assured her that she would still be a "technical virgin" for her husband, we don't know exactly what happened. Kemal dies in her bedroom after their liaison and that alone implies that Mary is "not pure" anymore. According to Cora, she is now "damaged goods". Mary knew the price of the loss of virginity even before Pamuk got the better of her "I'd be ruined if they even knew we'd had this conversation, let alone if they..." And if Cora does not help Mary hide the dead body of Pamuk - and Mary's secret, "I'll be ruined, Mama. Ruined and notorious, a laughing stock, a social pariah. Is that what you want for your eldest daughter? Is it what you want for your family?"

At that time, and even these days in certain cultures, virginity was the most sublime virtue a woman could offer her husband. It is supposed to be a "gift" to him. It's as if the success of the marriage rests upon whether the bride was still a virgin or not. (Think Lady Di who was chosen by the royal family as the suitable partner for Prince Charles instead of Camilla because Camilla was not virginal. And think of what happened to that marriage and the tragic/happy ending). It was assumed (and yes, men bought into this) that no (decent) man would take a non-virgin woman for a (decent) wife. But I think more than anything else, it shames the family that they had it within them to have raised a "loose" woman, loose here just means sexual or acting on her sexual feelings prior to the "blessings" of a minister who is supposed to be an agent of God.

This is sexism at its worst. Obviously, women lose their virginity because there was a man who "took" it. But the focus is on the woman who "couldn't wait". What about the (maybe virginal) women who married the non-virgin men? And yes, it is generally accepted that a man should not be a virgin when he marries.

So it was a scandal that Mary was not pure anymore. Never mind that there was a person who lost his life, not much emphasis on that. That may be forgiven as the show is from the point-of-view of the Crawley family, and everything should be done to protect her reputation. Her loss of reputation would mean the demise of the Crawley family and its estate perhaps. I'm sure to some extent, their love for Mary, who may be dismissed by society, is a concern of theirs and how that experience will be for a marginalized member of society.

Propriety and image to society was the most important thing. There is a scandal if there is even a trace of an impropriety.

Scandals and Secrets

Scandals and/or secrets define people. Robert knew that. He said to Carson "My dear fellow we all have chapters we would rather keep unpublished." Robert must be referring to how when he married Cora, he was not in love with her and although that was only true for the first year of their marriage, that is something he is not proud of – that his real motivation for marrying his wife was because of the money she brought in to their estate.

Little did Robert know that he was being protected from the knowledge of his own daughter, Lady Mary's scandal, by everyone in his family! I'm not sure what they are worried about if Robert knew. Would he disown his daughter? Is this so unforgivable a sin to a father by a daughter? Would he be shamed if he knew he was giving away a daughter at the altar with the scarlet letter written on her forehead? So instead of enlisting his assistance to help his daughter in distress, they keep the secret from him.

After realizing that Kemal had died in her bed, Mary panicked and employed the help of her loyal maid Anna. Anna then came up with a plan to move the corpse back to Pamuk's room but that the two of them would need extra help. And Cora, the mother of the scandalized woman, was the best candidate to help them. Cora is obviously shocked by the suggestion but then is convinced to help out after realizing what a huge scandal this would be and how Mary's reputation would be destroyed if they didn't. Cora later says that she can never forgive Mary. This condemnation from her own mother must have damaged Mary irreparably (if Mary was a real person!). Imagine your mother saying to you that you are worthless from her perspective from now on. And yes, some parents still have a black-and-white-only worldviews. You've made a mistake and so that's it. You cannot look good in my eyes for the rest of your life.

Cora is also worried about her own personal reputation. Aside from having a "damaged" daughter, she is also an accessory to a crime. But Mary hopes that in time Cora will be forgiving, just like any typical child who still longs for her mother's unconditional love. Cora promises to keep the secret from Robert to protect him. She also asks Anna to honor this secret.

When Matthew proposed to Mary, Mary decided to wait to give him her affirmative answer. She was debating whether to tell Matthew about her fling with Kemal Pamuk. She believed that not to tell him would be a lie, but if he later found out somehow, he would leave her. She was overwhelmed with shame and decided not to tell him. Matthew interpreted this silence as a rejection. Matthew felt that Mary did not really care for him and thought that since Cora was pregnant again, there was a possibility that Matthew would not become the heir, and so Mary was not eager to marry him. Matthew felt so hurt and rejected and planned to move back to Manchester. This was his way of rejecting Mary as well. Rejection is a pretty awful feeling. It is very wounding. And so when you are rejected, you tend to withdraw from the environment that has your perceived "tormentor".

Grandma Violet would later find out about the scandal. She was initially aghast and stern. But after some thought, she also fought for Lady Mary's reputation. "Everyone goes through the aisle with half the story hidden", implying that everyone, including herself, has some baggage he or she takes with him or herself when starting a new life. (Remember how she was also from the impoverished nobility!)

Carson had a secret too. He used to be a performer. He was being blackmailed by his former partner. He felt ashamed of his past. He has vanity and pride. He offered his resignation when found out and believed it was undignified to have had this history considering the position he has now.

Similarly, John Bates is keeping his own past in the dark. He is terse. He seems to be holding onto a secret but refuses to talk about it even to his girlfriend Anna. It turns out he has covered up his ex-wife's crime of theft, confessed to it, and was imprisoned for. The Anglo-Boer War also changed him: He was shaken and became an angry man. These days we may think of him as presenting with symptoms of PTSD (Post-traumatic stress disorder). To cope with this, he drank.

In all cases, it is the overwhelming feelings of shame and rejection that people are trying to avoid. That's why they hang on to secrets for as long as they could. It is understandable as these emotions are very painful.

Sexuality

There's no question that in that era sex was taboo. Cora and Robert still sleep in separate bedrooms and more, Robert is rather ashamed to admit that he joins his wife in her bed in the middle of the night.

Early in Season One, Mary was in love with an in-the-closet homosexual Duke. In the scene with her and the Duke in the servants' quarters, we can see how Mary was confused by her sexual feelings aroused at that time. They were in conflict with her idea of propriety and righteousness. She didn't want to be labeled "loose" or "fast" which were synonymous with sinful during those times. "Oh dear, if I answer truthfully you'll think me rather forward," Mary says to the Duke of Crowborough when he asked if she liked being alone with him. Imagine the guilt she must have felt about having yearning or sexual feelings alone?

A few episodes later, Lady Mary was smitten by Kemal Pamuk and his magnetism. She flirted with him while they were riding. But Pamuk became too aggressive and she was no match. And the taste of sex was too powerful to resist. And that led to their affair, Pamuk's death and of course the scandal. Had sex not been a taboo subject, the charge of that evening may not have been too strong for her and perhaps would have had a different ending (But we audience wouldn't have an interesting show!)

On the other side of the spectrum is Homosexual Footman Thomas Barrow. He is played by handsome Rob James-Collier who is straight in real life. Being homosexual during that period and what that means is really the narrative of Thomas - "illegal" – which means almost denying one's very existence. No wonder Thomas keeps asserting himself, desperate to be acknowledged, let alone the natural hormones doing their job and draws him to people he is sexually attracted to. He takes great risks to be acknowledged such as by making advances towards the Duke and Kemal Pamuk. You could be imprisoned if you made a pass at someone and they could report you during those years. "All my life they've pushed me around just cos I'm different." – This says it all about how Thomas feels about himself. He belongs to a despised and discriminated minority. He is oppressed. And when someone is oppressed, especially for a long time and has no way of breaking through, that internalized hatred, including self-hatred, can morph into rage that could explode. Or that seeps out to the people around him who become his target. And what's it like to have a secret like that? It must be dehumanizing.

Hierarchies and Power

Matthew and Isobel were middle-class and were snubbed by the aristocrats of Downton Abbey, especially Countess Violet when they first arrived. Even Robert did not think highly of Matthew's solicitor profession then. And although Mary did not love Patrick, Patrick had been raised around Mary; and that meant Patrick was from a better class than distinctly middle-class Matthew. Lady Rosamund, sister of Robert and aunt of Mary, reminds Mary that Matthew is only a middle-class solicitor, he's not rich or powerful at all, and that Mary will, "just be bored with him". Ultimately, Lady Mary decides to wait before giving Matthew her decision. Although her real reason for waiting has to do with her dilemma of whether to reveal her evening with Pamuk, her mother's unexpected pregnancy complicated it. If the baby is a boy, then Matthew will no longer be the heir, and Mary would simply be the wife of a middle-class lawyer.

Violet may be an absolutist in her values and beliefs, but she melts every now and then, especially towards family members. Keeping the circle of nobility tight was important to her so initially she was not in favor of Matthew as he was from the middle (lower) class. But she eventually learned to respect Matthew's integrity as she realized that that is virtuous.

Regarding the dynamics between Lord and Lady Grantham, Robert got upset with Cora when Cora was supporting Sybil's desire to be politically involved. Robert felt that his authority was being challenged, and this issue is a source of volatility for him. Aside from threatening his position of power, this is also a move towards separation from him by both Cora and Sybil. Of course at that moment, these were all unconscious psychological drives. But his behavior was spurred by them, bypassing his reasoned self. It is hard to lose a position of power and not be able to control perceived underlings especially after having this position for a long time.

By the end of Season 1, we can tell that Tom Branson, the chauffeur, and Lady Sybil have a budding romance-- which Mrs. Hughes' keen observant eyes did not escape--and of which she disapproved. She would say to Tom in the last episode with a look of disdain, "Be careful, my lad, or you'll end up with no job and a broken heart." Tom is young and idealistic. Mrs. Hughes is old and traditional, and propriety is her game. She believes that crossovers are dangerous and almost immoral. Actor Jim Carter, who plays the butler Mr. Carson, stated that Carson sees upstairs and downstairs as two completely separate worlds that should not mix.

Mrs. Patmore downstairs also does not like not having the keys to the pantry. Instead, she still has to ask Mrs. Hughes for them. She believes that as head cook, she should be mistress of her domain. So she feels frustrated that her power has limits and she does not see a way to fight it. So at times, her frustration comes out as anger towards Daisy, who is her subordinate. So Mrs. Hughes wields power over Mrs. Patmore, who in turn bosses Daisy around.

Thomas on the other hand senses that William is intimidated by him (And Thomas' own need for power or to dominate someone is in need of an object) he bullies William and makes him perform his duties. William has a crush on Daisy but Thomas sabotages his efforts to expose his feelings for her. William does not fight back but instead suffers in solitude.

All of the above shows us how people want positions of power and will cling to them for as long as they can.

Falling in Love

Matthew was snared by Lady Mary's beauty the first time he laid eyes on her. The look in his eyes and the dropped jaw gave him away. But before that, Lady Mary would overhear him saying that he did not want any of the Crawley girls to be pushed on him for marriage. Of course Mary felt insulted and used that to justify her repulsion towards Matthew initially. She coined the phrase "sea monster" to describe him and belittled his middle-class background. Matthew plays along with pretending to be undeserving of Mary's attention due to his lower class beginnings. Well, of course we know that that stage was their flirtation. What happens at this time is there is some discomfort about being attracted to someone, especially if you are not sure if your feelings will be reciprocated. (In psychological lingo, the risks of being rejected by your idealized "object" are still too high.) So as self-protection, you send out signals that you are not that interested until you get some feedback that the other person may be interested. It hurts to be rejected!

They have chance encounters in the neighborhood. During dinner you could tell that Matthew is subtly letting Mary know that he's interested. But Mary stuck to her pride for awhile and pretended she was not interested. But once Matthew is out of sight or perceived by her to have "distanced" again, she worries and pines for him. This is the typical oscillating distancer-pursuer dynamic that gets played out in unstable relationships.

But Mary and Matthew eventually fall in love. Matthew slowly befriends Mary and then pursues her and she succumbs. Right before Matthew proposes, Mary thought she noticed that her youngest sister Sybil had her eye on Matthew after Matthew saves Sybil from harm at a rally. She teased Matthew that her sister may have a crush on him. Matthew then fished to see if Mary had feelings for him too by telling her that she cannot be accused of having a crush on him. To which Mary hesitated to respond … and the kiss transpired and the rest is history. Such is the game of love!

Matthew proposes in 1914, right before Season 1 ends. But Mary is confused and does not give Matthew an answer. She believes she needs to reveal to her future husband what happened between her and Kemal Pamuk, and that she is not virginal anymore. But shame overcomes her, afraid that that revelation will drive Matthew away.

With the Lady Edith and Sir Anthony Strallan match, this is still very unstable as Edith seems to be partly drawn towards Sir Anthony to show Lady Mary that Edith is also desirable, rather than embracing Strallan because Edith is truly in love with him. Strallan may have fallen for Edith's attentiveness towards him and prematurely felt ready to propose to Edith at the end of the season. Although it was malicious of Lady Mary to lie about Edith and an imaginary suitor, it is probably best that these two don't commit to each other yet.

In terms of compatibility, it's not surprising that Lady Sybil would be interested in Tom. He is handsome (played by Allen Leech). He is driven and ambitious ("I won't always be a chauffeur"), intelligent and articulate ("Politicians can't often recognize the changes that are inevitable"), and most of all he and Lady Sybil have a common cause that give meaning to their lives. (It's been said that Bill Clinton fell in love with Hillary Clinton's mind). He almost found a twin in her with his life goals of promoting social justice. There is a psychological theory called Self Psychology that asserts that sometime during our life – usually much earlier, and before we can tolerate the different "others" - we are looking for a twin, a mirror that reflects especially the good in us. And that strengthens our ego and fosters the agency within us that tells us we have power to be in charge of our destinies.

When we are passionate about larger-than-life issues, we are drawn to people who hold the same or similar values. Perhaps we are on some unconscious level aware of the immensity of the work we want to accomplish and realize we need a helper. It's the "we-ness" experience, you and I together against the world. What better helper to have than someone from the other side of the aisle?

There is another important love story going on...

"It's always sad when you love someone who doesn't love you back. No matter who you are", Anna quips to Mr. Bates. She is open and expressive, including about her budding feelings for Mr. Bates. Mr. Bates on the other hand is cautious and secretive. He likes Anna but is protecting her from his own history (which he perceives makes him unworthy of her love) and how that might affect Anna's life. But Anna cannot hold back her feelings anymore and one time confronts Mr. Bates about his secret and then reveals her own feelings for him: "Because I love you, Mr. Bates. I know it's not ladylike to say it, but I'm not a lady and I don't pretend to be." Anna is my favorite character. She is so real and honest.

Simultaneously downstairs: Like any young infatuated girl, Daisy thought that Thomas was the embodiment of everything that is good in a human. She does not know yet that Thomas is gay. Julian Fellowes says: "When you're young you simply select people you are physically attracted to, and then invest them with all sorts of qualities which they probably don't possess." We call this 'idealizing transference' in psychology. It is the need to connect with the 'idealized object'. "I'll do anything for you," she says to Thomas. So when she was enlisted by O'Brien and Thomas to frame Bates regarding a stolen wine bottle, she joins them. She is naïve and quite indifferent to everything else that's happening around her except for those things that affect her personally.

We're irrational when we are in love, as simple as that. Not knowing that someday we will pay a price.

Friendships

Mary's "friendship" with Anna is solid and Anna is loyal. True friendships are not class-based. Mary and Anna almost have similar issues in their lives and that strengthens the bond between them – they both love someone who seems unreachable. We see that in the evenings especially when Anna is brushing Mary's hair, that is when they share their lives with each other.

Some other interesting friendships in the show:

John Bates supports William's love for Daisy as he knows what it's like to love someone who seems unattainable. He has brotherly warmth towards William and wants to be William's confidante. Mr. Bates tries to reach out to him, but William shuns his efforts. (It's interesting that it is Bates who is trying to get William out of his shell when Bates himself is hiding in his own cocoon.) Perhaps growing up an only child, William is not used to sharing – especially his inner life. Or that no one was interested. William seems to be a neophyte in the ways of love: "I was just wondering why we get so drawn to people who have no interest in us. What's nature playing at?" and a question posed to Mr. Bates one time: "But you can't make someone love you, can you?"

Another interesting pair: "Life's altered you, as it's altered me. And what would be the point of living if we didn't let life change us?" says Carson to Mrs. Hughes after she confides to him about rejecting a suitor one more time. Carson shares his wisdom with Mrs. Hughes. There is a special bond and genuine caring between these two top dogs. They have respect for each other. Also Mrs. Hughes is maternal to Bates and William. She said to Mr. Bates after discarding a brace that he thought would correct his limp: "We all carry scars, Mr. Bates, inside or out, and we must all put up with them as best we can. You're no different to the rest of us. Remember that." That encounter was a good combination of tenderness and tough love. To William, Mrs. Hughes encourages him to pursue Daisy and to not let Thomas push him around. Mrs. Hughes looks out especially for William, who is often melancholic due to homesickness and Thomas's bullying.

And then there is O'Brien who uses her relationship with Cora. She tries to get the latest gossip from Cora and manipulates her. She knows that Cora trusts her, like they were "friends". It's understandable how a strong bond forms between a lady and her maid as they spend considerable time together. And since the maid pampers her ladyship, it creates a safe environment for her ladyship to talk. O'Brien stated falsehoods about Bates and others to get them fired. She gossiped about the goings-on upstairs to the servants downstairs and especially to Thomas. She is not close to anyone, even Thomas is more just a "partner in crime". She does not seem to like any of them. The only back story we have is that she had several siblings. She is an angry woman, perhaps betrayed by someone who was dear to her; therefore she is cautious about getting close to anybody.

On the other hand, Mrs. Patmore is single-minded. Her only interest is her meals and the kitchen. She is always ordering Daisy and keeps her on a tight schedule. She may have Daisy's interest at heart and is maternal to her but she certainly does not know how to show her tender side to her. Remember that tenderness can go a long way sometimes so don't be miserly with it to people you care about. It relieves stress and makes you more connected especially during a difficult time.

Jealousy

Violet was looking for a replacement for a maid and asks for Cora's help in finding one. O'Brien misinterprets that Cora was looking to replace her and O'Brien felt threatened. So she saw an opportunity to strike back while Cora was bathing one time. O'Brien slid a wet bar of soap on the floor next to the bathtub intending to have Cora slip when she got out. At the last minute though, Sarah O'Brien felt pangs of guilt and ran to the bathroom to stop it. (This is the only time we see O'Brien's vulnerable side. Other than that, she seems to be a one-dimensional character. She is a scheming vendetta-wielding person.) It was too late, and Cora slipped and had a miscarriage. O'Brien will feel this guilt for the rest of her stay at Downton and becomes a fiercely loyal servant to Cora.

In Episode 4, we can see that Lady Mary resents father's budding closeness with Matthew. She was starting to fear that Matthew will become "the favorite child". She senses that Matthew, being male, has something that she can never offer her father (aside from being the potential heir). This contributes to her upset feelings that her father wouldn't fight for her and her inheritance by trying to break the entail.

At one point, Mrs. Patmore felt threatened as well. Before she left for eye surgery, Mrs. Patmore instructed Daisy to sabotage Mrs. Bird's (Temporary filler for Mrs. Patmore's job) cooking as she was afraid that she would be replaced by Mrs. Bird permanently. This job is all she has got and she can't lose it. Daisy obeyed Mrs. Patmore's suggestion but made a mistake and got caught. As always, Daisy is a good person and felt the need to confess. Mrs. Bird consoled her when Daisy started crying. Daisy became like a child who was caught doing something wrong, scolded publicly and then felt remorseful. The other servants were also forgiving.

Jealousy or feeling replaceable is one of the most excruciatingly painful experiences. It could morph into something dangerous and make the threatened person do vicious things.

Aloneness

Due to her failing vision, Mrs. Patmore kept making mistakes, and one time she mistook the salt for sugar, which of course, was catastrophic. She felt so ashamed and then blamed Daisy for the mistake instead of admitting her impairment. She uses Daisy as a punching bag. She has trouble admitting her weaknesses as she is insecure within herself, and her job is the only thing that gives her meaning. Nothing is scarier for her than losing her job.

When she was left alone by Anna in the hospital right before her surgery, Mrs. Patmore wept, and we saw her vulnerable side for the first time. When she became aware of her existential aloneness, she must have been overwhelmed. She had NO ONE at a time when she could have used a companion. She keeps herself busy and distracted when at work in Downton Abbey, so she does not have to get in touch with her solitariness. She may also be warding off potential rejection, which is, of course, a very stinging experience. She does not appear to have family at all, and she tends to alienate her co-workers back at Downton as she is so demanding especially with Daisy. She is mean but that is also her way of shoving people around her from getting close to her. She is what we call "counter-dependent". She is very much like Violet.

Thomas, being an outcast due to his homosexuality, also experiences aloneness. He is forced to live a secret life and even with his "best friend" O'Brien, he cannot admit his "otherness". Feeling alone and/or different make some create a wall around them even more as exposing the need to be connected can feel even more dangerous as it may mean opening one's self up for potential rejection. Which one is more frightening?

Trauma

Trauma stays in the body unless you process it. "If you think she'll recover from carrying the body of Mr. Pamuk from one side of the house to the other, then you don't know her at all....When she dies they'll cut her open and find it engraved on her heart." Mary responds to Anna's inquiry regarding how she is recovered after the death of Kemal Pamuk. (It's interesting that she was talking about herself in the third person. As if she was trying to prevent a gush of emotions). Mary is telling us that she has not recovered at all and perhaps will never recover from the trauma she experienced that night. Trauma gets some people stuck in the past as a part of the brain is literally "hijacked" by the flood of stress hormones. So unless that part of the brain holding on to the memory gets "released", the anguish stays.

Although she has a way of carrying herself that does not show that Lady Mary is suffering inside, according to writer Julian Fellowes, Mary is more vulnerable and open after this trauma and has shed her ice queen persona.

Daisy was also the one witness to Kemal Pamuk's corpse being carried into his room by Lady Mary. She did not see Anna and Lady Grantham helping Lady Mary. She was traumatized by that visual and was bothered by any references to his death afterwards. She is usually torn between being moral and pleasing her superiors. She was intimidated by Lady Edith's social position; that's why she revealed to her what she saw. But perhaps she also saw this as an opportunity for release of her angst – some form of catharsis - and Lady Edith was happy to be Daisy's "savior" at that time.

Grief

Towards the end of Season 1, William's mother became deathly ill. His mother did not want him to be concerned and be distracted from his work and so William was not informed on purpose. Fortunately, Lady Mary, who learned from Isobel about William's mother's condition, had a soft spot in her heart for William and his mother's situation. Mary thought that not being able to say goodbye to a dying parent was not acceptable. Lady Mary revealed his mother's condition to William and encouraged him to visit her before it was too late.

William came back to work soon after the funeral. He was obviously still affected by his mother's passing as one time he got into a brawl with Thomas when he deemed Thomas insensitive to Lady Grantham's miscarriage. Perhaps Lady Grantham's grief tapped into William's own grief and brought it to the fore. The aggression towards Thomas was an energy that had been building up for a while anyway and that incident was the straw that broke the camel's back.

It is also interesting to note that William's mother did not want him to know about her serious condition. Perhaps because death had been a constant companion in that household with all of her other children dying in childhood. His mother was trying to prevent William from experiencing more sorrow. To her, that is an expression of love. We parents do try our very best to shield our children from painful experiences.

Mrs. Patmore also has a take on grief: "Nothing makes you hungrier or more tired than grief", noting William's change in behavior as well as implying she knows what it was like to experience this powerful emotion. This is uncharacteristically revealing of Mrs. Patmore.

Losing a parent and the grief that goes with that is one of the most powerful emotions a human being can experience. The anger that surfaced in William is a natural stage of grief that most people go through. Changing eating habits such as over or under-eating is also a symptom of grief. It is the body's way of re-grouping after a dramatic unhinging juncture.

Emotional Expression

Englishmen are known for their stoicism. In monotone, Robert Crawley said, "I love you" to his daughter, Lady Mary, when she was questioning him why he was not sticking up for her. He admits that this was hard for an Englishman to say. Robert is protective of his family, but it seems like his most tender moments are reserved for his servant "family" downstairs. He had no qualms forgiving Carson after Carson's confession of stealing from the kitchen to shush a former fellow performer about to expose Carson. Robert's compassion was also aroused another time, and he rescinded his decision to fire Bates. He also paid for Mrs. Patmore's eye surgery when she starts to go blind.

Robert has vulnerable emotions but always tries to contain them, consistent with how the males were expected to behave during that era, especially the English. Emotional containment was part of their code of propriety. But he wept in Bates' presence after finding out that Cora had miscarried a baby boy. He then apologizes to Bates after exhibiting his painful feelings: "I'm sorry. I don't mean to embarrass you," as if he did something that was inappropriate. These days, we just think that it's natural for someone to be affected deeply by a tragedy, and to express that is not objectionable.

Robert is not the only one who puts up an emotional façade. I say façade because no one is really emotionally invincible. People just learn how to hide their emotions.

"He flatters me. I'm tougher than I look," were the first words said by Violet Crawley in Season 1. She seems to be insulted that her own son was worried that she would not be able to handle the news that the Titanic sank, and that Patrick Crawley, heir apparent to Downton Abbey, is dead and so once again the future of Downton Abbey is uncertain. Perhaps her own son knows that deep inside the tough façade that she presents in public, she is a crumbling cookie.

People who appear or who like to appear emotionally invincible may have deep-seated feelings of insecurity inside. From the back story about Violet that we know of at this point, she came from the aristocracy and married an aristocrat, yet her family-of-origin was quite impoverished. So she must have felt like an outsider with her in-laws (Later we will find out that her in-laws were also not as well-heeled as she thought they were). This must have triggered feelings of not-belonging, and thus insecurity for Violet.

Violet does not let her guard down as that would mean exposing her true self and then trusting someone to take care of her. That must have been a very scary concept to Violet as she needed to hide her true (impoverished – and insecure) self from the world. She needed to pretend that she was one of them, and so she developed a tough persona, lest she would be "found out" and then be abandoned.

Cora to Violet: "I know you have rules, and when people break them, you find it hard to forgive". Violet also grew up in the Victorian era, and Cora's valuation about her above encapsulates the essence of the stereotypical Victorian. Propriety of behavior within one's class is paramount. So showing vulnerability, let alone allowing one's self to feel vulnerable, was taboo in that society.

It's hard to get close to someone who presents such a façade. It is sad if that is your mother or father. As we can see, Violet's children, Robert and Rosamund, are not particularly close to her. Very seldom also do we see Violet hugging or embracing even the young women of the Crawley brood. In fact, we see Robert quite annoyed by Violet and even trying to beat her at her own game. He engineered Isobel to become co-chairperson of the board of the hospital, unbeknownst to Violet, as he wanted to teach Violet a lesson: Share power.

To mask Violet's feelings of insecurity - and aloneness (When you feel insecure, you don't usually feel like you have an ally and therefore you feel alone), Violet acts tough. She allows no one to get close to her and get to know the core of Violet. When she became a widow and matriarch of Downton Abbey, she savored the power that went with it and she made this power ubiquitous. She used this position as a cocoon that she spun around herself to keep everyone at bay by intimidating them.

Violet either alienates or dominates everyone else in her generation especially Cora's mom, Isobel and even Dr. Clarkson. Her disdain for Isobel may also be related to the fact that Isobel is the mother of the new heir of Downton which means Violet will lose Downton to Isobel eventually, and thus her position of power, and as a result she won't have a cover for her humanity anymore.

Rigidity

Violet exhibits this attribute of rigidity. It's almost expected that she is old-fashioned--and a snob. She's lived a very cloistered life. It's also hard to be the only one in your generation left and feel like there is no one else who shares your views and beliefs. Of course that will make you want to defend if you feel outnumbered. You would want to dig in your heels to protect yourself.

Violet is easily threatened by anything from outside her cocoon and thus she is anti-America. Because of not having been exposed to any other lifestyle than being part of the aristocracy, she is unable to understand other people's world views such as why Gwen would even desire to leave the life of service and ambition to become a secretary. When her cook was leaving to get married, she asked "How can she be so selfish?" She does not understand why women would want to have more rights, or why electricity and swivel chairs are even necessary inventions. Keeping the status quo is her goal, as this is how she can keep her much-treasured power. Thus she had some trouble with Sybil's involvement with the women's rights movement as well. She experiences others' autonomy as a personal affront or threat.

Robert, on the other hand, has his inconsistencies. He is kind, generous and protective of his servants and the lower classes. But at times, he is slow in embracing new values if they officially creep into his own family members. For example, he refused to allow Lady Sybil to get involved with the women's rights movement until he realized that maintaining this stance might mean losing his own daughter.

Role Players

Raised by parents who grew up in the Victorian era, Robert is a role-player and hangs on to tradition as much as he can. Like the way his mother was emotionally (and physically) detached from him, he seems cold and distant to his own daughters. In monotone, he said, "I love you" to Lady Mary when she was questioning him why he was not sticking up for her. He implies that although he does care about her, his perceived duty to save Downton Abbey always comes first. When he said, "I have given my life to Downton, I was born here and I hope to die here. It is my third parent and fourth child. Do I care about it? Yes, I do care!" he had more emotion in his voice. (Who would he be without this estate?) He decided not to fight the entail as that would mean abandoning Downton if the money were separated from it. No wonder Mary questioned his devotion to her.

His marriage to Cora was a marriage of convenience. Downton Abbey was in financial distress and only his matrimony to a rich heiress could save the day. At eighteen, he tied the knot with American heiress Cora Levinson, age twenty, and even though he had genuinely fallen in love with her after the first year of marriage, for the rest of his life, he would be gripped with guilt for what he thought was dishonesty. So when he grasped that the Duke of Crowborough's intentions to wed Lady Mary were because of her presumed inheritance, he castigated him. (In psychological lingo, this is called "projection" – imputing to others, qualities we can't accept in ourselves.) And when he sensed that Lady Mary and Matthew Crawley were falling in love, he encouraged the romance as he knew in his heart that what's right is to marry someone only for love.

What about Cora's role? It is interesting to note that Cora single-handedly decided that Robert should not be in the know regarding the scandal surrounding Kemal Pamuk's death. She was more concerned as to how this was going to affect Robert rather than enlisting his assistance to help their daughter. I am speculating that a father's image of his daughter as virginal is so sacred, that a sex scandal destroys the father as well. After all, he is supposed to "give away" with his blessings a pure daughter at the altar. Her impure status demeans him as well and may arouse feelings of disgust towards his daughter. Hence Cora tries to prevent both father and daughter from experiencing such feelings, preventing and protecting Robert from experiencing hurt and shame.

From the moment we meet her, Mary is always being set up with men to marry (either someone with money or to an heir of Downton Abbey) and it seemed like that's her role in the family – to save Downton Abbey. Her life is not hers. Mary doesn't look like she is happy or enjoying life. She was being set up with her cousin Patrick who drowned with the Titanic. But she didn't really care for him and didn't warm up to the idea of wearing mourning clothes. You can tell she wants to do right for her role but resents it. She confessed to Carson: "Have you ever felt your life was somehow slipping away? And there was nothing you could do to stop it? The odd thing is I feel, for the first time really, I understand what it is to be happy. It's just that I know I won't be". Lady Mary dislikes her life and wishes she had a job to go to like Matthew. "Women like me don't have a life. We choose clothes and pay calls and work for charity and do the Season. But we're stuck in a waiting room, until we marry." How sad. But this must have been women's (from the aristocracy) role before the women's movement.

Carson, too, plays a "role". The Crawleys of Downton Abbey are the only family Carson's got, and he feels insecure himself if Mary is not going to inherit it. He is also a father-figure to Mary, perhaps more so emotionally than Lord Grantham himself. If Mary loses Downton, he is also out of a job. Like Lord Grantham, Carson has difficulty accepting change and takes great pride in Downton Abbey and what it symbolizes. He is like the alter ego of Lord Grantham. He is strict and protective of the Granthams and he does not tolerate his staff bad-mouthing them upstairs crowd. Mrs. Hughes thinks he reveres them too much. "Everything matters". That explains Carson's attention to details. He reprimanded William regarding a torn garment. To him protocol is important. "We've all had a smack from Mr. Carson", Daisy consoles William. He wants them all to show proper conduct. He believes people should live and work by certain standards and gets very upset whenever the standards are disrupted or breached by his coworkers or subordinates. He is the patriarch among the servants and admonishes them if they veer from the straight and narrow path. Carson is a man who takes his job seriously. But despite his steely persona, he can be avuncular to some of his wards. He was initially against the employment of Mr. Bates due to his disability. But Bates grew on him, and Carson later admitted he could not imagine Downton without Bates.

Similarly, Mrs. Hughes is the matriarch downstairs. But she can separate her emotions from the family drama going on upstairs. She is a professional. Every now and then she questions whether she should have pursued a different life than a life of service. Like working in a shop, marrying, etc. She knows the personalities of the servants intimately just like a devoted mother. She is also strict like Carson, rule-based, like a drill sergeant and slave driver. She is indifferent to the women's rights movement. Perhaps she realized that she will be too old when the fruits of this movement are ripe.

Self-esteem

Lady Sybil has a healthy self-esteem and was not offended when Branson criticized the British aristocracy of which Lady Sybil is a part of. She knew where her efforts belong: "Because it's gloomy things that need our help. If everything in the garden's sunny, why meddle?" She is her own person and puts her money where her mouth is. Perhaps being the youngest and left to her own devices, she developed a strong personality.

Tom, her future beau, is not an opportunist. In fact, I think he is sincere. He has an above-average self-esteem compared to most of the other servants. He didn't hesitate to comment on Robert Crawley's book collection during their first meeting. And he saw an opening in Lady Sybil's burgeoning interest in politics and lit her fire. He was comfortable to engage her in conversations while driving her around. Lady Sybil was also fascinated by his openness and freshness. His good looks and intelligence probably served as magnets for people's attention so that was a foundational component of his self-esteem. We don't know anything about the quality of his relationships with his parents and family members so I will only speculate that those were relatively healthy.

The Cottage Hospital became a forum for Isobel to actualize her desire to help others. She's eager and zealous and exudes self-confidence. She persuaded Dr. Clarkson to try out a treatment for a farmer who was suffering from dropsy (and she succeeded). She insisted on giving Molesley a chemical from the hospital for what she thought was erysipelas (red skin caused by bacteria). With this second incident, she was almost cocky – and she was wrong. Violet says to her: "You are quite wonderful, the way you see room for improvement wherever you look. I never knew such reforming zeal." Isobel replies: "I take that as a compliment." Isobel was very educated and not from an aristocratic family, so perhaps Isobel was not confined to roles. She felt the freedom to pursue her dreams. Perhaps as a widow with no desire to remarry and her only child grown, her time is hers and she uses it as she pleases. She's been a "liberated woman" and has broken the glass ceiling (relatively speaking) even before the women's rights movement. She is untraditional and does not believe in following authority that she does not respect. She likes to challenge Violet's position like in the flower show when she questioned Violet's automatic wins.

When Isobel's son Matthew arrived at Downton Abbey, he was appalled that there is a grown man assigned to him whose job is to wait on and dress him like a "doll". He detested having a valet. "Seems a very silly occupation for a grown man", he describes the valet's job. Moseley, the valet, was offended by this. Matthew did not see the point of having a personal valet until he understood from Robert's explanation that a valet – and any worker in general - takes pride in his job and this pride enhances their self-esteem.

Matthew is confident and very much his own man. He has strong opinions and insisted on having a job as soon as he arrived at Downton Abbey. He takes no orders from anyone. He means what he says and says what he means. He does not look up to the upper class and does not think they should look down on the lower classes. As a solicitor, he could perhaps have tweaked something to break the entail and have Mary inherit Cora's money. And even though he is the bottom line benefactor of this law, it is because of his felt duty to honor the law that he does not toy with it.

John Bates is the equivalent of Matthew downstairs (In the same way that Anna and Bates are like Mary and Matthew upstairs). Although there is a suggestion that he may have led a checkered past, he has integrity. "I couldn't take your money, m'lord. I can take wages for a job done. But that's all" John Bates said to Robert when Robert was firing him and Robert offered him some money before leaving. Bates also caught Thomas stealing wine but did not tell on him. In fact, Thomas tried to frame Bates as the thief. Bates respects his co-workers and thinks that if in the future, he is in a predicament (not necessarily immoral), his co-workers would help him out.

And then there's Anna who does not think of herself as a "Lady" but lives by her own rules, at least in terms of her emotional and romantic life. She has enough self-esteem to challenge O'Brien. "Fight fire with fire," she said to Bates when O'Brien tried to make Bates the fall guy for some missing cuff links.

Gwen, the young ambitious servant also has pretty good self esteem. We see that she is not afraid of progress and technology. A woman who is not afraid of technology at that time was quite unusual. Remember she bought a typewriter with no qualms. One time, she made a comment to Daisy when Daisy seemed intimidated by the task of turning on the light. "It's electricity, not the devil's handiwork. You'll have to get used to it sooner or later ".

So you can see that class is not the necessary ingredient for healthy self-esteem. Although coming from a financially secure environment makes a huge difference and especially the presumed dignity that automatically comes with that. But being raised in an emotionally secure environment trumps most other parameters of self-esteem.

Adaptability

If Matthew was reluctant to adapt to their new lifestyle, his mother Isobel was eager to prove to the Granthams that they deserve to be treated like one of them. She was willing to take on the traditions and trappings of being a member of the aristocracy. But it turns out that that is not an end in itself. Isobel is a social worker at heart, and she wants to use her position to carry out causes that benefit the poor and the powerless, the downtrodden and the underdog. In other words, she is politicizing too.

Over time, Matthew comes to accept his life in Downton. Initially he was reluctant to concede that his life had changed and so must he. However, as he comes to help Robert run the estate and learns about his new role, he grows to accept –and enjoy - his fate.

Many times during our lives, we kick and scream when we're handed a situation we weren't asking for. Our tolerance for frustrating situations may be lower than others. This could be situational or perhaps we were frustrated too many times too long, especially in our young life, and that energy has morphed into anger. Fortunately at times, those situations turn out to be golden opportunities.

Ambition

Most of us do not venture easily out of our comfort zones. Why not? As the road to any life-changing destination can be twisty and turn-y, Gwen Dawson, a maid, gets discouraged every now and then. She wonders if she'll ever get her prize. Early on, Gwen was told that because she was JUST the daughter of a farmhand, she was LUCKY to have gotten a job as a maid. That message must have haunted her during those times of doubt "I was born with nothing and I'll die with nothing," she uttered bitterly. At another time, she said to Lady Sybil : "Forgive me, m'lady, but you don't get it. You're brought up to think it's all within your grasp, that if you want something enough it'll come to you. But we're not like that. We don't think our dreams are bound to come true, because they almost never do." Privileged people do not understand how their upbringing alone (raised by successful people in a more-or-less secure environment, at least financially) is an asset for them compared to underprivileged ones who grew up in environments of doubt.

But is it the chicken or the egg? Gwen must have had the drive and ambition to achieve, which was lit by a discontent with the status quo. It is possible that she was raised in an environment where her caregivers and other family members were not threatened by her independent spirit. So she felt free to venture out of her socially-defined boundary and comfort zone.

Gwen was also lucky to have two women be ardent supporters of her dream to become a secretary. Her roommate Anna supported her in this quest for a different life. Although Anna does not harbor a desire to leave service like Gwen, she does not stop Gwen from pursuing her dream nor question her. Anna simply does what she can to help Gwen further down her road. Gwen describes Anna as "like a sister". Girlfriends sometimes are more apt to support each other than real sisters as they don't have the history of rivalry growing up and living in the same household, fighting over the same set of resources.

Best of all, Lady Sybil becomes her most consequential ally in achieving her dream. Lady Sybil encourages her when she is losing hope, searches for a job for her and gets her an interview. On top of that, Lady Sybil takes her to the interview and lends her a suit. Lastly, she writes her a letter of recommendation.

Disability

When the servants first laid eyes on John Bates, they immediately noticed that he was holding onto a cane. We could tell that they, except for Anna, were concerned. Not concerned for Bates that he might be in pain or uncomfortable, but concerned that lame Bates would not be able to perform his duties as a valet to the family patriarch well, if at all, and that perhaps they would be saddled with more to make up for what Bates was unable to accomplish. Thomas (who wanted this valet job) and O'Brien actually try to sabotage Bates and try to define him as an invalid who can't function.

Co-workers, although caring for each other most of the time, are also sometimes uneasy when they feel like they've been passed-up by another, especially if they believe they are more deserving of the promotion. And, yes, some can be vicious like Thomas and O'Brien. They worry that there won't be enough or anything left for them if others get more.

Aside from his own life inconvenienced by his disability, Bates is also aware of how his co-workers see him as undeserving of his position, and he must detest the feeling that goes with that. So he tried to correct his limp by wearing a brace that proved to inflict more pain than help.

Conclusion

I hope you have enjoyed reading my musings and perhaps learned something new about the inner workings of the human psyche.

The Season ended with the outset of World War I. Mary is still without a flame and therefore her parents and Violet are apprehensive (and we the audience are in suspense) as to how they can keep Downton Abbey. We await the fate of Lady Edith and root for Sybil and Tom, Anna and Bates; perhaps even Daisy and William. What then when the feminist movement matures and the Irish Republican cause catches interminable fire?

There's Season Two and I hope to enlighten and entertain you some more in the future.

Bibliography

Masterpiece: Downton Abbey, Season 1. [Video] Prod. Masterpiece Classic, 2010.

Fellowes, Julian. Downton Abbey Script Book, Season 1. William Morrow Paperbacks, 2013.

Fellowes, Jessica. The World of Downton Abbey. St. Martin's Press, 2011

About the Author

Louella Chapman is a practicing Marriage and Family Therapist in California. She is an avid fan of Downton Abbey.